BLUE SKY PRESS
Santa Monica

—

In Her Own Right

CHELSEA MADELINE

Design by Alex Cohen

Blue Sky Press
A division of BLUE SKY BLACK SHEEP
www.blueskyblacksheep.com

Library of Congress Cataloging-in-Publication Data
Names: Madeline, Chelsea
Title: In Her Own Right
Identifiers: LCCN 2024944545
ISBN : 978-1-7369469-0-9

Design and illustration by Alex Cohen
Jacket art by Raymond Woog, 1927

For my mama,
Joyce Lynn Burnham

CONTENTS

IN HER OWN RIGHT

Isabelle Meyer	Cleopatra	Guggenheim
Judy Blume	Jane Eyre	Lee Krasner
Sylvia Plath	Virginia Woolf	Beatrix Potter
Eve	Françoise Gilot	Georgia O'Keeffe
Sylvia Beach	Sappho II	Phillis Wheatley
Sappho I	Hilma af Klint	—

BEFORE ALL ELSE, YOU ARE YOURS

MY GOD HOW SHE SHINES

Toni Morrison	Simone Leigh
Frida Kahlo	Taylor Swift
Deborah Levy	Athena
Reese Witherspoon	Beyoncé
Jamaica Kincaid	Maya Angelou & Oprah

CREATOR OF BREATH AND SOUL

In our early days of parenting, a new dynamic emerged—a dynamic of negotiation. My love and I bartered for more sleep and alone time, time to create and time to work. All the intangibles became scarce, and we had to figure out how to share them.

It was challenging to convince myself my writing was worth commandeering the family's hours. My consulting work, sure. It made sense that I would "get" that time and my partner would care for our baby then—for that work paid dollars today, a tangible and sure resource we'd put in the family pocket. But writing was different. There was no guarantee my words would ever be published, let alone make any money. But I knew, all the way inside myself, in order to continue to be myself, I needed to be writing.

This collection is my exploration of the resources needed to make one piece of art, let alone a body of work over the course of a life, and the cost, both personal and cultural, of not making that work.

I thought if we could see the exchanges we were having not as insular and one-off, but part of a larger, gendered, and historied pattern we'd be able to hold ourselves differently within them. We'd know changing the dynamic in our minds and our homes was a meaningful step toward changing the dynamic culturally.

I hope the stories of these women help to carve space for the art you're meant to make.

IN HER OWN RIGHT

Isabelle Meyer had been watching her family from the wall for nearly a hundred years, watching as her son raised his daughter, that daughter raising a daughter of her own. And one day, after reading the words in this very collection, that daughter took Isabelle's painting off the wall to see what words lay behind it, what the painter had said about his mother as he preserved her in oil.

What she found was this:
MME. *Jules Comte — merè du peintre.*

It was his mother and yet, he left her nameless, referenced only in relation to a third husband and him, her son. He said nothing of the sculptures she carved in her study, nothing of the salons she held, nothing of the daughter she raised into a poet, nothing of the woman she was. Everything but Isabelle's piercing gaze has dissolved, but Jules is still here, penned to the canvas.

Their stories aren't given an hourglass as ours are, sand slipping through until all traces vanish. No, their stories stay, the ink living longer than the breath in the bodies of the people who worshiped a woman. It distorts what we know of every moment that came before this.

We think they lived quiet. They roared.

Judy Blume's husband said she was *allowed to write* as long as it didn't interfere with raising the children and keeping the house. He said it only took paper and pencils to keep her happy, no need for a credit card to Saks Fifth Avenue like the other wives. He said it like a pat on the head.

He was a *very busy professional*, so she raised her children herself. And though she wrote book after book—thirty, she wrote thirty—he didn't read a single one. "I didn't care," she says now, her eyes resigned, but defiant too. She divorced him at thirty-seven, thank the heavens, finally awake enough to see her own magic.

She kept his name after she left, I assume because it was hers when she became famous. I wonder if she wishes she was still Sussman, the name she grew up with, or if she wishes she could make up a new one entirely or take George Cooper's name instead, that sparkly-eyed gentle soul. But thirty-seven years later, she's still dragging John's name around the world, making it glow.

She asked us what we were taught about Sylvia Plath. No one hesitated: *crazy, suicidal, an unfit mother*. They recite it to us in the rooms we're meant to learn in: *Here is what women have been. Here is what women are.* (Can you feel your smallness? Have I done my job?)

Do you want to know the true story of Sylvia? She was prescribed a medicine, illegal now, that altered her mental state. She realized what was happening before it was too late and got off the medication. Years later, needing a prescription again, her doctor ignored her when she said*, It can't be this one. Anything but this one.* He gave her that one. She did not survive it.

She had us raise our right hands, hundreds of women together, as we swore: *I will tell the true story of Sylvia Plath to everyone I meet.* She said she was recruiting an army to correct the record.

She reminded us stories determine who we call crazy and who we call *genius*.

I asked Chat GPT about the women in the Old
Testament. It described them the same, all the way down
the list: *mother of, wife of, sister of.* It wasn't until I balked
that it relented:

Eve, not wife of Adam,
but first woman created by God.
Can you feel her divinity now?

Chat GPT tells me Sappho's work is fragmented because *she wrote on perishable materials that do not stand the test of time*. Causation is a thorny thing. I say, *surely Plato wrote on papyrus too?*

Yes, it says, but scribes copied his works onto more durable things like vellum. Thirty-six remain, fully intact more than 2,000 years later. I say, *It sounds to me like the paper wasn't the problem.* It's the decider who determines which voices we let linger.

But I keep thinking about those students of Sappho's, for she had them too, just as Plato did. I wish they'd taken up the role of preservationist, digging a library cave and lining it in stone, carving her poems into the walls, making a map to the crypt that they'd tattoo on their hip, passing it along to their daughter when she was of age, their granddaughter after her, so no matter what war the men were fighting and how broken the land became, her words would still be there breathing.

I wonder in what way we're still doing this now. Guarding his work from the elements as we let hers decay, saying all the while—*she did write it on perishable material.*

The name Cleopatra comes from a Greek word that means *glory of her father*. The title she adopted later, Theā Philopátōra, means *goddess who loves her father*.

It makes me think of the Bechdel test. To pass it, a film must have two women characters (with names) who have a conversation about something other than a man. In other words, the film must make us the center of its world, if only for a moment. It must recognize that together we are a complete universe, a constellation unto ourselves.

She said we're more likely to credit other people when we make a thing. *I keep wanting to talk about how we did this together*, she says to her editor. This, she says, is the result of the deadly sin of pride. We deflect to keep ourselves likable, unthreatening.

> Maybe this is true.
> But maybe we just see the webs that link us.

Maybe we know that *Ulysses* wouldn't have come to be without Sylvia Beach and Shakespeare & Company. Joyce wouldn't have had the money, and his eyes wouldn't have held out without the doctors. He needed her to publish it when no one else would. He needed her to figure out how to sneak it into America once it had been banned, tucked into suitcases under trousers. We wouldn't know a thing about Molly Bloom without Sylvia.

Yes, we know all about webs.

Virginia said Shakespeare couldn't have been a woman because a woman in that era wouldn't have had enough time to write that many words on a page between all the chores assigned to her, because she would have had to hide her books, stolen from her brother's shelf, beneath her embroidery, because she would have been laughed away from the theater's door. I boycott Shakespeare on principle.

There is a trend of women talking about childcare in their books or in the interviews that launch them. *I couldn't have written this without my mother, who I paid a living wage to care for my four children as I sat at my desk with the door closed to every want and need and whoop and cry. / I put on silencing headphones and wrote these words. / This book is only possible because my husband took a year off unpaid to care for our baby. / Our nanny is the only reason you can hold this book in your hands.*

In every one of these notes, they draft the permission slip we didn't need but were waiting for anyway: *you are allowed to create, even now. In fact, you creating will make this world better for them. It will soften it; it will brighten it. Do whatever you must to make it possible.*

It will not make you bad.

I tell my grandmother what Virginia said, and she tells me that when she was supervising the accountants full-time and mothering two babies, she used to spend her only week of vacation each year washing all the windows and screens.

It was the only time, she said. *It had to get done.*

I tell her she should have booked herself a flight to Greece. She laughs.

The headline said: *Françoise Gilot, Artist in the Shadow of Picasso, Is Dead at 101.* They called her *an accomplished painter in her own right.*

In her own right means they're going to do it, the thing they ought not do, they're going to spin you a web of every man she ever loved or spoke to. If she touched pinkies with him as they passed on the sidewalk, they'll likely mention it here, in her obituary.

In her own right means she almost stood on her own two feet before they kicked them out from under her. Before they gaslit her with every word. Before they transposed his image on top of her art.

In her own right means half of the lines in her obituary's opening paragraph are about him. *In her own right* means he was a shadow she couldn't shake, that once she looked him in the eye no one could see her unwarped again.

Picasso knew it would be like this. He taunted her with it as she walked away.

> "You imagine people will be interested in you? They won't ever, really, just for yourself. Even if you think people like you, it will only be a kind of curiosity they will have about a person whose life touched mine so intimately."

Doesn't it sound like a curse?

She said something about trying to make it a "hardworking book." Otherwise, she said, why publish it at all? It needed to have some larger meaning, some moral, something beyond just the honest telling of her life.

I wonder if it's only women who feel this way when they sit down to write. Who feel like it's their job to say something universally applicable, to make their poetry sit like self-help. If even in our poetry we're meant to martyr, then there's nothing in this world that is just for us; then we have nowhere to be free.

Sappho wrote in questions. *"Who wronged you, Sappho?"* They scoff at young women who speak with rising intonation. They tell us to stop *asking*, to start *telling*, to eradicate the interrogative. To *speak like we take ourselves seriously*. And I suppose it's because if you leave it open ended, someone else answers for you. But what a shame if that makes us speak as if there is nothing left to wonder about.

When we're talking things through she'll often say: *This is a question that I have to answer.* Only then will she tell me the question. When this happens I know she doesn't want outside voices to intrude with solutions. She just wants the space held for her suspended curiosity.

I hold it.

Hilma af Klint believed the spirits gave her a commission. During a seance they channeled her visual messages, and she was to paint them, to share them with everyone— the secrets of the universe. She didn't question it. She got to work.

She knew the collection was meant to be shown in a temple, and she sketched the building she saw—a spiral that went up and up and up. No such building existed.

As she was dying, she told her family to box them tight, every one of her pieces, for twenty years. To show them to no one for at least that time. By then, she thought, human consciousness may be ready for them. She knew she'd lived too early.

Her first solo show was held at the Guggenheim seventy-nine years after she died — in their main exhibition space, a spiral going up and up and up, just as Hilma had envisioned, just as she had drawn, more than a decade before the Guggenheim was conceived.

What is the difference between *having a vision* of a building and *designing it*? I suppose design claims the power lives within us, in our hands and our minds, while *vision* acknowledges that everything ever created has been a collaborative endeavor between us and everything not us, that we originate very little of all this, that, if we're lucky, we just catch the comet as it falls.

The word *genius* used to mean the spirit of a land, but then, at some point in history, we assumed it for ourselves, sure if we'd made or said anything of note, the genius must live within us; it must *be* us.

Frank Lloyd Wright was paid 1.5 million dollars in today's money to design the Guggenheim. Hilma died with twelve hundred to her name. If the genius lives within you, it makes sense that you would be compensated well for bestowing it upon the world. But how do you compensate for a channeled vision? Is receptivity worth the same as "genius"?

Phillis Wheatley's poems were erudite, sophisticated, merging Greek mythology with the Bible, laced with Latin. The deciders were sure no one would believe a woman of West Africa, kidnapped and living enslaved, would have the capacity to weave such words.

Their solution was simple: they'd need eighteen (white) men to testify on her behalf, to say, *Yes, yes, it seems to me these were indeed penned by the poet.* Her words couldn't belong to her until three Johns and two Samuels swore it to be so.

Meanwhile, there was a woman in England, Selina, the Countess of Huntingdon, who took her own money, money she could have otherwise spent on gowns and soirees the town would talk about all season, and used it to print Phillis's words onto the page. Without Selina would I hold a copy of these poems now, 250 years later, or would they too be scattered, written on material too perishable?

The word patron comes from the Latin *patronus*, which means protector or defender. I can't help but imagine a circle of women dancing, swords in hand, defenders not of life but of legacy, who, with every effort put toward preserving another woman's art, proclaim, *She is too important. I will not let you forget her.*

When Lee Krasner moved to the Hamptons, she and her husband, Jackson Pollock, each needed space to paint. I don't know how the conversation went, how they decided who would go where, all I know is that Pollock took the barn, and Lee was left with a bedroom.

His work could be as vast and encompassing as it wanted to be, and it did want to be vast, while she, in the little bedroom, painted a series called *Little Images*. When he died, she moved her studio to the barn.

Finally, *space*. A year later she painted the swoops of green and spheres of pink in *The Seasons*. It's almost seventeen feet long — a consuming flash of color — one of her best-known works.

We too are like goldfish, expanding until we meet the edges of the space that sustains us. I don't know how the conversations go or have gone, all I know is, *the barn is meant to be yours*.

I was assigned only one book that spoke in the voice of a woman through all high school. I can tell you about Hamlet and Huck Finn and Holden Caulfield, Piggy and Nick Carraway, but the only woman's voice we got to hear was Jane Eyre. (Of course the one book we got has a crazy wife locked in the attic.)

Years later I learned of a prequel of sorts written by Jean Rhys. It colors in the wife's backstory: she is Creole, born in Jamaica. Her family loses their wealth and she's married off, shipped to England where she is surrounded by people who are nothing like those in the place she calls home. She descends into the underworld of her mind. There's always a reason for anything that rings to them of insanity. I remember now we also read The Yellow Wallpaper, another woman descending into madness. Were we told that it was about the author's postpartum depression? Did we study what postpartum depression is and how it has gripped women through the ages? Were we told to ask our mothers what it was like for them and cautioned about what it may hold for us?

I don't think so.
I just remember us saying she was nuts.

Beatrix Potter was a scientist. We don't think of her this way. We remember her for watercolors of rabbits and such for children. But she studied mushrooms too. They didn't care to see her research until after she died. Twenty-six years later they published a compilation of her studies: *Wayside and Woodland Fungi.* This reminds me of a line that caught me as I read the paper last night:

"She's a giant," said so-and-so, a curator of photographs at the museum. *"In 500 years, people will be talking about her work."*

I keep wondering if he meant to leave out the word *still.*

Georgia O'Keeffe drew these abstractions that made you feel as though the garden of one stem was going to swallow you whole. She was trying to show us how much there is to *feel* if only we look. She was trying to tell us we never look.

It was almost time to show her body of work, but her lover had his show first. His show: photographs of her body unadorned, her gaze piercing. The critics decided *this* must be who she was, it must be all she was. A body unadorned. A woman free.

When it was her turn to hang work upon the wall they said, *Ah, of course, she drew the world between a woman's legs. We should have known this would emerge from her. After all, did you see those photographs?*

Her lover, who was also her art dealer, fanned their embers. Their assumptions trailed after her as she went on. Eventually she decided enough was enough. She decided to tell them what it was to her, to stop letting them write her story. *While some claim these paintings have erotic overtones,* they write on her website, *this idea was dismissed by the artist, vehemently, for six decades.*

The word *canon* comes from a Greek word meaning ruler. *This is the stick we measure against; here's how we determine if a thing has merit.* Our primary criterion seems to be how resilient a work is to the changing of seasons, the shifting of worlds. The longer it's lived, the more heft we assume it has. But there's a cost to weighing things toward the ancient—you move into the era when most of us were expected to be awfully quiet.

A school's syllabus has hardly changed in the past hundred years: Plato and Ovid and Homer and Chaucer and Frost and Descartes and Nietzsche and Fitzgerald and Hemmingway and Kafka and Dickens and Joyce and Salinger and Melville and Orwell and Steinbeck and Whitman and Sartre and Shakespeare and Tolstoy and Proust and Faulkner and on and on. If we're lucky they throw in Emily and Toni and Virginia and Jane.

They decided these are the people whose work you must know if you are to be considered educated. But what of the one who studies Claudia Rankine and Joy Harjo, James Baldwin, Ocean Vuong, and Rachel Cusk? Their bodies of work are considered *extraneous*, not the very foundation of wisdom.

If the things we are taught in classrooms create the window through which we see the world, should we not be able to say: *Your view is distorted, I'd like a wider lens. Zoom out, zoom over, there's more to see here.*

I keep thinking about that word *extraneous*. It comes from a Latin word that means *something or someone outside of a particular group*. It only came to mean *irrelevant and unnecessary* later on.

The deciders, of a *particular group*, decide what is critical and what is extraneous. They point and say, *this* is the thing of importance. *This* is where you should strive.

But what if we said, that land looks barren, swampy, bumpy. Why would I ever go *there*? I see another land lush with fruit that will juice down my chin, drip down my arms; I see a land dancing in butterflies, everything waiting for me. Keep your gesticulations for someone else. I have my own compass; it never leads me astray.

We are the new deciders.

BEFORE ALL ELSE, YOU ARE YOURS

What if you took everything ugly and hid it in the cupboard and bought a ceramic vase and filled it with orange poppies.

What if you hung the portrait of Simone but you didn't let yourself be nostalgic about it. You didn't fawn over a bygone era, but instead you whispered an incantation every morning: *some young woman, in some distant time, will tape a picture of me beside her desk to remind her of her lineage.* What if then you write the words she'll underline after she's put her baby to sleep.

What if you never utter the word wife again but only *Chelsea* and wear your ring on your first finger to remind yourself that before all else, you are *yours*.

The days can pass without you filling the space of your body and they often do. But what if you got back in there?

They leave and I sit on the porch counting the times I see the word 'wonder' in the newspaper. They leave and I pull the lamp outside to keep reading after the sun's gone. They leave and I pour myself another thimble of Malbec.

They leave and I learn how to make a cappuccino in our machine. (The espresso spurts violently the first time. I mop up the kitchen and try again.)

They leave and I buy myself a bikini and swim in the pool, face underwater, as fast as I can. The breast stroke always reminds me of my mama. It's what she raced.

They leave and I read Annie Ernaux beside a flickering candle. I drink pineapple smoothies and squeeze all the juice out of the tangerines. I make hibiscus tea and drink it so cold it's almost frozen. They leave and I stare in my eyes long enough that I can see me again.

Sometimes I see how long I can stay quiet
when I sense that every word I say aloud
betrays me.

It makes me
grinnier than I am,
giddier than I am.

It takes the soul and depth
out of the way ideas live
when they stay inside me.

I hope you post so many things you love every day that only your mother and the boy who loves you make it to the end of your three-thousand slide story.

I hope you underline every one of your books with such abandon that they are illegible to everyone after you. I hope you write full monologues in the margins.

I hope you get the juice every day. And the cappuccino. And the quiche. Get one for her too. I hope you send the text message afterwards that says what you feel but what no one ever says:

I find you enchanting.

I hope you tell every one of them they are your sisters. What good is it to keep that to yourself? Who knows the hundred ways you'll save each other over your lifetimes.

MY GOD HOW SHE SHINES

The word power comes from the Latin *potere*
which means *to have the ability*.
(This is also the origin of the word potential.)

I asked DALL-E to paint me a picture of a table of women, heads of all the countries in the world, coming together in a space of collaboration and unity. It painted them wearing white linen, lit by torches of fire, women of every color, one holding a baby. I stared at my screen until the sun set and my husband found me sitting in a dark room.

I had never been able to conjure it for myself, but the AI doesn't have the indoctrination I do. To it, leadership can look like us.

When Toni was hired at Random House she could've said, *Here is the box I must now live within. I must acclimate. I must adapt.* They had their way of picking projects, a certain direction in which their eyes were trained. She was looking the other way entirely. She said, *There's a whole library of books you don't even know to nurture, to midwife to this plane, but oh how hollow that shelf looks without them.*

She called Angela Davis and coaxed her memoir out of her. She cupped the words of June Jordan and Lucille Clifton, pouring them onto the page. She knew *Corregidora* would become part of the canon.

Toni gave us eleven novels of her own, but she did something else too. She built a bookshelf no one in that world seemed to see needed filling, and upon it she slid the words and worlds of Black women. She pushed aside the coats at the back of the wardrobe and showed them there was snow.

If they're all looking north
but every bit of gravity
you've ever encountered whispers
east, east, east,
go east, child.

Set up a bench,
a bookshelf,
a banquet.
Build the world that only you can
see is coming and wait
for them there.

I keep thinking about Frida's monkey. About how if she'd thought: *I want a pet* her mind would have begun scanning for animals filed as such. She would have ended up with some blue-eyed kitten. We're told this is how we find our way to the things we want in life, to the person we're meant to be: we envision it and set out to get it.

But her friend gave it to her at a party unprovoked, goodness knows where he got it, and rather than scoffing it off or finding the local zoo, she took him home and loved him fiercely.

I'm not sure what this is meant to tell me. Surely not *love every wild thing that gets passed your way*. But maybe: *everything enchanting will come to you by happenstance.* If the world only knows who you are, if you tell them clearly enough, they will know just the thing to shower upon you.

Tell them who you are.

Deborah Levy says she's looking for a major unwritten female character, a woman who has desires she does not suppress, a woman who *steers her high horse.* She keeps pitching these characters to film executives, and they keep responding with a smile and a shake of the head. *No, no,* they say, *they need a woman their audiences will like.*

Their audiences like women who ensure everyone else's needs are met and pretend they have none of their own. It is no small thing that she keeps pitching these characters, ignoring the easier option: To sell them the version of womanhood they've decided to echo. To pretend women are smaller than they are.

It means the home Deborah yearns for, the one with a rowboat and a pool and a fountain, the one she'll share with her daughters, recedes further into her imagination with every meeting—for securing material things in the tangible world requires behaving by the rules of the deciders, performing upon the stage they erected.

Except when it does not.

Reese played the bend-and-snap law student. A man called Robert directed the thing. She performed the deciders' version of womanhood for two decades, slowly accumulating the resources to revolt.

When she did, she was ready. In ten years she produced *Wild*, *Gone Girl*, *Big Little Lies*, *The Morning Show*, *Little Fires Everywhere*, *Truth Be Told*, *Daisy Jones & the Six*. These are stories of women setting off to find themselves, women binding together to defend themselves, women making mistakes and making lives of creativity and autonomy. These are real women, messy and glorious. Deborah ought to leave those film executives, whoever they are, and go for a swim in the Santa Monica sea with Reese. A constellation unto ourselves.

I've spent months trying to define *power*. This is the closest I've come to something that feels true:

They executed Socrates because they claimed he was a *poet or maker of gods.* They said he didn't pray to the state-sanctioned deities. He asked too many questions. He didn't believe in the godhead of the sun or moon like other men and instead believed the sun was stone and the moon earth. How many years later would he have been heralded as the premier astronomer of the era, hypothesizing that the moon was made of matter. But in 399 BC this wasn't yet the framework of things, so they made him drink hemlock. It meant death to ask the questions he did.

Each era has a tone and tenor, a palette that brings it to life, that gives it color. We live *inside* the color of our age and, from within, it gets hard to remember that it's not that everything is that color, it's that we are given a pair of lenses tinted the hue of our generation. Figuring out how to take them off and see the world in its raw state is a nearly impossible feat.

Maybe power is just the ability to impact the color of the age. To keep everyone in their crimson lenses or fade us into the indigo era.

The verb to *name* comes from the Old English *nemnan* meaning to *designate*. It's the way we control what something can be, what it can become. We categorize it, boxing it in with language.

The way the Frenchman Louis Antoine de Bougainville was leading an expedition in Brazil, six thousand miles from home, and there in this land not his own his officer found a plant, a bright, bold beauty of a shrub, and named it in *honor of his commander*, a way of planting flags around the psyche of the world, filling our mindspace and wordspace with them, the way two hundred and fifty years later we still carry his name in our mouths: *bougainvillea*.

(Jamaica taught me this.)

She knew if she was to write, if she was to say anything she needed to say, she needed space from the person she had been yesterday, from her family back on the island, from everyone who *knew her so well*.

With this space she could become something new, something not different than herself but *more of herself.* So she set aside the name her mother had given her, Elaine Richardson, and claimed the one she bestowed upon herself:

Jamaica Kincaid.

Simone Leigh was selected to represent the United States at the Venice Biennale. She built towering sculptures of women and added raffia to the roof. These things were expected of her, but she did something unexpected too.

She said, *Now that this door has been opened and I stand here inside, let us throw open every shutter, every blind, every window. Let us make this a space where they can all join me.*

Across the lagoon, she created an addendum to her installation called *Loophole of Retreat*, a symposium of Black women, artists and scholars, poets and activists, who gathered to present their bodies of work at the same moment guests from all over the world were flooding the Biennale across the water. It was as if she was saying,

Let my name not be the only one etched here. Let it be remembered that we were here together.

Taylor told them she wanted to own every song she'd ever written. She wanted to hold her name in her own pocket. She wanted to buy it back.

Instead, they sold it to a man called Scooter.

She thought about it for two months and decided this would not do. She began recording all six of her albums over again. She held her life's work in her hands and announced: *This thing here is no longer where the magic lives. This pile is ashen, still smoking, let it lie. I'll spin you a new spool of gold. It will hold more than the one before, for this one will live free from the moment it's born.*

The word *mentor* comes from *The Odyssey*. Homer wrote that while Odysseus was away fighting, always fighting, his friend Mentor came to advise his son.

We began to say his name when we meant passing wisdom from one generation to the next, when we meant cultivating the spirit of the world that will follow ours. *Mentor*.

But here's the thing — Mentor was actually Athena in disguise. She took a shape she knew he'd listen to, a shape he'd respect, so her wisdom would sit as it ought. So her words would ring as true as they were. What shape does a woman's wisdom take? Is it *potential* or is it *power*?

They both come from the same seed, growing in opposing directions from there, one above the ground, one beneath. Inverses of the same weight, the same might, one basking in sunshine, the other living buried.

There was a person Beyoncé was supposed to be, a person she thought she was, but it was a different self entirely who showed up on stage, sang as she did, performed to the thousands of eyes waiting to watch her. She must have felt fragmented, two things in one body. So she gave the other part of her a name: Sasha Fierce.

Sasha was fearless, sensual. Like a whisper from somewhere ancient, something untaught, by which I mean something true. For a time this was how she let herself be both: the thing the world expected a woman to be and the artist she was.

I often think about that first time Maya Angelou spoke with Oprah on her show *People Are Talking*. How she must have looked into that young woman's eyes, for Oprah was only twenty-four at the time, and seen the spark and fire that burned within herself.

She must have seen that they emerged from the same creative waters, and in that moment, which was just a publicity stop, like so many publicity stops she made over the course of her career, she decided *yes, HER*.

From that moment until the day she died Maya was devoted to Oprah, as Oprah was devoted to her. A kinship not of blood but of spirit, two women co-creating self and destiny and legacy.

CREATOR OF BREATH AND SOUL

In the very beginning, god was a woman.

They didn't know how conception worked, so it
seemed a miracle when a woman became pregnant,
like she was summoning life from another realm,
pulling it here by sheer force of will. She was a
portal, a mystic, a creator of breath and soul.
All life emerged from her body.

Of course She was god.

She went by many names, often Divine Ancestress, the furthest-back grandmother at the beginning of time, the woman from whom all people emerged.

In their temples they housed snakes, creatures of wisdom, and maybe just maybe, in ceremonies late into the night, the venom of the creature would show them visions and make them speak prophecies.

They'd stand together under the fig tree, passing around a branch of the fruit, the body of their goddess. The first communion was theirs.

For these women, sex was a sacred act, not in opposition to their reverence but part of it, as close as one could get to divinity on earth. Her body was not something to hide from; it was her way in.

These women were independent, powerful, free, rooted to the minerals of the earth and descendent from stars. Their babies took *their* name, inherited *their* land, *their* home, *their* world. This was the way of things for ten thousand years, maybe more, and then suddenly, violently, everything changed.

In they came from the land we now call Russia, the light-haired ones who had learned to make war chariots and so thought they were mighty. They rode into the lands where women stood tall and decided something must be done.

Their attack was subtle at first, a simple revision to the story. *Don't you know,* they said, *our god destroyed your goddess. It is right here in the tale. He was mightier than her. The strongest of them all.* They pointed to the page as they scribbled in their lies. They knew the power myth had to tint the world a particular hue.

The stories told in the land began to shift; a new cast of characters introduced, new dynamics unfolding between the beings of the otherworld.

When they continued to pray to the goddess, the invaders tried a new strategy. *Our god says he's the only god,* they said. *He told us to kill all those who worship another. He said massacre is the only way.*

They passed word around town that there was to be a ceremony in the goddess' temple; they packed it full of her believers, men, women, and children alike. They killed everyone inside.

The women who remained saw that the invaders worshiped control not creation. They lived on a different plane entirely.

They saw just how far they'd go to eradicate all whispers of the goddess, grandmother to them all. They began whispering very softly, praying only when hidden. Things began to change for the women. Their purses taken from their hands, their names scratched from their lands, their husbands' scrawled in their place.

In this new world, if a man raped a woman, she would be punished for it. The whole town could stone her — to death. He could now have as many lovers as he chose, while she would be banished if she so much as gazed into the eyes of another. The circumference of her world shrunk smaller and smaller and smaller until even her body belonged to him.

Everything the light touches is our kingdom.
Nothing, nothing, nothing is yours.

The invaders saw it was working, the world morphing as they'd hoped. They pressed on. Now we must destroy every trace of Her. Your temples must crumble, your statues turn to dust. No evidence can remain.

Humanity must forget Her.

And for the most part we did. Thousands of years later archaeologists, all bred in the church of the invaders, found Her statues buried deep in the soil.

Don't worry, they said. *It wasn't the religion of the land. It was only a cult. A strange little pagan cult. Women doing devil-like things upon a hill. How eerie, how awful. Thank goodness the invaders came and showed them the way to the light, the way to goodness.*

How many times must we be gaslit before we say *enough*.

end.

Acknowledgements—

This book wouldn't have come to be without Kim Agnew and the magic she nurtures inside the lean-to. Thank you to Alex Cohen for holding the book's design as sacred and to Shona, Jess, Chris, Esti, Kristen, and Meg for tenderly holding early iterations of the project.

There are several women whose writing and teaching formed the foundation of research for this book and to whom this collection owes a debt of gratitude:

Chelsie Diane and her class *Poems and Power*
Katy Hessel's *The Story of Art Without Men*
C.S. Merrill's *O'Keeffe Days in a Life*
Merlin Stone's *When God Was A Woman*
Davino Pardo & Leah Wolchok's film *Judy Blume Forever*

And most ardently, thank you to Pete, Theo, and this little soul growing inside me for making the everyday shimmer. Thank you for helping me create a life and home within which there is space to be writer and mother both.
I love you so.